The Word Became Flesh
The Original Stageplay

Christian Playwright

Copyright © 2019. Christian Playwright. All Rights Reserved.

Christian Playwright asserts the right to be identified as the Author of this work.

Please be advised that this document serves solely as a reading version of the script. Any reproduction, distribution, adaptation, or public performance of this work without the express written consent of the author and/or the owner of the production rights is strictly prohibited and may result in legal action. Interested parties may seek to acquire said adaptation, performance and/or production rights by contacting the Publisher, HCP Book Publishing, at info@hcpbookpublishing.com.

ISBN-13: 9798856263052

Published by:

TABLE OF CONTENTS

Characters 4
Setting 5
The Story 6
Play Details 6

Act I
.... 8
SCENE 1 9
SCENE 2 14
SCENE 3 16
SCENE 4 19
SCENE 5 22
SCENE 6 25
SCENE 7 28

Act II
.... 31
SCENE 1 32
SCENE 2 37
SCENE 3 41
SCENE 4 44
SCENE 5 48
SCENE 6 51

CHARACTERS

MALES

Voice of God

Jesus

Isaiah

Micah

Zachariah

Priest I

Priest II

Gabriel

Joseph

Plump Man

Innkeeper

Mark

Paul

Raymond

King Herod

Adviser

Balthasar

Caspar

Scribe

Simeon

FEMALES

Nevia

Micah's Wife

Elizabeth

Anna – Mary's mother

Mary

Maurine

Anna - Prophetess

EXTRAS NEEDED

SETTING

ACT I

SCENE 1 - Home setting (include table and stool)

SCENE 2 – Same as Scene 1 (Add bed)

SCENE 3 – Street Side

SCENE 4 – Temple Setting

SCENE 5 – Outdoor

SCENE 6 – Indoor

SCENE 7 – Same as Scene 6

ACT II

SCENE 1 – Outdoor (include doors Stage Left & Stage Right)

SCENE 2 – Same as Scene 1

SCENE 3 – Outdoor (exclude doors)

SCENE 4 – Kings Palace

SCENE 5 – Stable

SCENE 6 – Temple

SCENE 7 – Same as Scene 4

THE STORY

The play begins with a conversation between Jesus and the Voice of God in which Jesus pleads for the souls of humanity and negotiates a plan to die in their place - to become the perfect sacrifice for the sins of man.

We are then transported 700 years before the birth of Christ to hear the Prophet Isaiah speak God's Word to the people of Israel about a coming Savior, and the Prophet Micah tell exactly where the Savior would be born.

Moving forward several hundred years, Mary is pregnant with Jesus, visits her cousin Elizabeth who is pregnant with John the Baptist. They share of the miracles in their lives propelling us through the days and events leading up to our Savior's birth.

PLAY DETAILS

Length: 60-90 Minutes
Cast: 20 Males, 7 Females, Plus Extras
Audience: Teens & Adults
Genre: Biblical Drama

THE SCRIPT

Act I

The Choice

SCENE 1

SPOTLIGHT COME UP ON JESUS

VOICE OF GOD: My Son!

Jesus stares out into the audience.

JESUS: You can't just destroy them, Father.

VOICE OF GOD: They have sinned. The price for sin is death, You know that.

JESUS: There must be another way. I know You love them as much as I do.

VOICE OF GOD: My Son, We created them in our own image. We gave them everything. They could eat from every single tree, except one. Only one. They have disobeyed.

JESUS: Look at them, Father, look how sorry they are. Walking around moping and repenting.

VOICE OF GOD: They must reap what they sow.

JESUS: I know the rules, Father. But rules can be broken.

VOICE OF GOD: At what costs?

A beat.

VOICE OF GOD: You are not responsible for the choice they have made, and there can be no atonement for sin without the shedding of blood.

JESUS: My Father, you hold the keys to all doors. Everything that is, or ever will be is Yours, and I have asked You for very little. But this one thing, I must ask.

VOICE OF GOD: Make Your request, My Son.

A beat.

JESUS: If You love them, as much as I do, let Me die in their place.

VOICE OF GOD: You are My only Son.

JESUS: Would You sacrifice Your only Son to save the world of man?

Pause.

VOICE OF GOD: Give me some time to prepare the altar.

A beat.

FADE SPOTLIGHT

Isaiah's Prophecy

ISAIAH, the prophet, enters wearing pajamas and carrying a torch lamp.

He puts the lamp above a table and sits around the table. On it are many scrolls along with a pen in ink. He takes the pen and dips it in ink as he rolls out an empty scroll to write.

NEVIA (Isaiah's wife) enters, also wearing her nightgown.

NEVIA: Its two o clock in the morning, Isaiah. Please come back to bed.

ISAIAH: I have had enough sleep.

NEVIA: You had another dream, didn't you?

ISAIAH: Yes.

NEVIA: The same one?

ISAIAH: Yes, and more.

NEVIA: Is that cause enough to deny yourself some well-deserved sleep?

ISAIAH: I must write the things that I have seen, and heard.

NEVIA: Haven't you written enough?

Isaiah chooses not to comment.
Nevia takes up one of the scrolls. She glances at it.

NEVIA: When did you write this?

ISAIAH: Last night.

Nevia reads from the scroll.

NEVIA: Nevertheless, there will be no more gloom for those who were in distress. In the past he humbled the land of Zebulun and the land of Naphtali, but in the future he will honor Galilee of the Gentiles, by the way of the sea, along the Jordan-

The people walking in darkness
have seen a great light;
on those living in the land of the shadow of death
a light has dawned.

You have enlarged the nation
and increased their joy;
they rejoice before you
as people rejoice at the harvest,
as men rejoice
when dividing the plunder.

> For as in the day of Midian's defeat,
> you have shattered
> the yoke that burdens them,
> the bar across their shoulders,
> the rod of their oppressor.
>
> Every warrior's boot used in battle
> and every garment rolled in blood
> will be destined for burning,
> will be fuel for the fire.

ISAIAH: I still love to hear you read.

NEVIA: Your hand is shaking.

ISAIAH: I am burdened, dear wife, with the knowledge God has entrusted me with. I am yet to get used to the idea of being worthy to be counted as one of His scribes.

NEVIA takes the pen from Isaiah's hand.

NEVIA: I will be your scribe tonight.

Isaiah gets up from the table, and Nevia takes his place.

NEVIA: What did you hear, and see this night?

Nevia writes, as Isaiah dictates.

ISAIAH: For to us a child is born,
to us a son is given,
and the government will be on his shoulders.
And he will be called
Wonderful, Counselor, Mighty God,
Everlasting Father, Prince of Peace.

Of the increase of his government and peace
there will be no end.
He will reign on David's throne and over his kingdom,
establishing and upholding it

with justice and righteousness
from that time on and forever.
The zeal of the LORD Almighty
will accomplish this.

NEVIA: Do you know what this means?

A beat.

ISAIAH: It means GOD will leave Heaven and come to Earth as He promised our ancestors He would.

NEVIA: Do you think this will happen in our lifetime?

ISAIAH: We can only hope, my love. We can only hope.

Nevia rolls up the new scroll and adds it to the collection. They take the lamp and exit.

SPOTLIGHT COME UP ON JESUS

VOICE OF GOD: My Son, a way has been made; the time and place decided.

JESUS: Where?

VOICE OF GOD: Jerusalem. Home of my chosen people. The center of the earth. If You are ready, I will make the announcement.

A beat.

JESUS: I am ready, Father.

FADE SPOTLIGHT

Micah's Prophecy

SCENE 2

LIGHTS UP

Micah jumps up out of his sleep. His wife is awaken by his sudden movement.

MICHAS WIFE: What is it, Micah?

Micah goes to a nearby table and rummages through the scrolls there.

He finds a specific one and rolls it out. He reads silently, taking it all in, his expression slowly lights up.

MICAH: It's starting to make sense now.

MICHAS WIFE: Micah, what is it?

Micah hands her the scroll.

MICAH: Read this!

MICHAS WIFE: Its three o clock in the morning. My eyes are still sleeping.

MICAH: How can you be thinking about sleep at a time like this? We are participants in one of the greatest events this world will be witness to.

MICHAS WIFE: You know, Micah, I never quite understand what you are talking about.

Micah takes back the scroll and reads.

MICAH: Marshal your troops, O city of troops,
for a siege is laid against us.
They will strike Israel's ruler
on the cheek with a rod.

But you, Bethlehem Ephrathah,
though you are small among the clans of Judah,

out of you will come for me
one who will be ruler over Israel,
whose origins are from of old,
from ancient times.

MICHAS WIFE: A ruler? Out of Bethlehem? Nothing good has ever come out of Bethlehem, Micah.

MICAH: Until now. Isaiah saw the event, but I have seen the place. The Messiah will be born in Bethlehem.

A beat.

MICHAS WIFE: I'm going back to bed.

She lies down in the bed.

MICAH: We will not know the true value of these Prophecies until we see it with our own eyes. My God, I count myself among the lesser of your prophets and yet you have counted me among the greatest by showing me these things. May Your perfect will be done here on earth, as it is done in Heaven. Even so, come Emmanuel.

LIGHTS OUT

John's Parents

SCENE 3

LIGHTS UP

ELIZABETH ENTERS carrying a water pot. She stops to rest her feet.

ZACHARIAH meets her along the way. He takes the water pot from her.

ELIZABETH: You were supposed to meet me along the way.

ZACHARIAH: I thought that's what I am doing.

ELIZABETH: Our home is right over there. I had to carry this water pot for three miles.

ZACHARIAH: I'm sorry, Elizabeth. I tried to leave sooner, but they were casting lots to see which priest would go to the temple to burn incense.

ELIZABETH: There are 20,000 priests, Zachariah. What are the chances of you being chosen?

ZACHARIAH: I was chosen this time.

ELIZABETH: To do what? Clean the altar and prepare it for the fire?

ZACHARIAH: No!

ELIZABETH: Kill the morning sacrifice and sprinkle the altar, the golden candlestick and the altar of incense?

ZACHARIAH: Not that either.

Pause.

ELIZABETH: There is only one thing left.

ZACHARIAH: Then that must be it.

ELIZABETH: You were chosen to burn incense?

Pause.

ZACHARIAH: Yes.

ELIZABETH: I'm not in the mood for your jokes, Zachariah.

ZACHARIAH: I am not joking this time.

Elizabeth's frustration suddenly turns to joy. She hugs him.

ELIZABETH: This is a lifetime opportunity for us, for you. Who knows what God will tell you there or what supernatural experience you will have. God has finally smiled on us. Maybe now He will favor us enough to give us a child.

Zachariah turns away saddened.

ZACHARIAH: We shouldn't punish ourselves with such hope.

ELIZABETH: Why not?

ZACHARIAH: Look at us, Elizabeth. We are old. Old people don't have kids or can't have kids for a better choice of words.

ELIZABETH: You are a priest in God's house. Where is your faith? Don't you preach that God can do all things?

ZACHARIAH: I have accepted that it is His will that we remain fruitless.

ELIZABETH: You can't ask me to accept that.

ZACHARIAH: I am not asking you to. But you should.

ELIZABETH: Do you know what it is like for a woman to be barren? To be labeled a mule?

Pause.

ELIZABETH: Promise me you will not give up praying and making a request to God for us to have a child?

Pause.

ELIZABETH: Promise me, Zachariah.

ZACHARIAH: I promise.

ELIZABETH: Say the words.

ZACHARIAH: I promise to keep asking God for a child.

ELIZABETH: Thank you.

Pause.

ZACHARIAH: All this talking has made me hungry.

Zachariah takes the water pot.

ZACHARIAH: You should prepare something easy and quick.

ELIZABETH: When will you go to the temple?

ZACHARIAH: The day after tomorrow.

ELIZABETH: Take time to prepare yourself. The presence of the Lord is not something to be taken lightly.

ZACHARIAH: You just want to hear me say I'm going on fasting, so you don't have to cook.

ELIZABETH: I never thought about that, but now that you mention it ---

ZACHARIAH: Don't even think about it!

They exit.

LIGHTS OUT

The Announcement

SCENE 4

LIGHTS UP

Zachariah enters with two Priests walking on his left and right. They enter the holy place.

One priest set the burning coals on the altar, while the other priest arranges the incense.

Both priest then leaves and stand outside the temple to wait for Zachariah.

Zachariah bows to pray for a moment.

He takes coal and put on the altar, followed by incense. He then bows to pray again.

ZACHARIAH: God please don't be angry with me for making my request known, but my wife still believes you can give us a child. If at all this is possible, don't hesitate to bless us, if You see us as worthy in Your own eyes.

Gabriel enters and stands at the right side of the altar.

Zachariah opens his eyes and falls back when he sees the angel standing there.

ZACHARIAH: Are you a priest?

GABRIEL: No.

ZACHARIAH: Then how are you able to stand in God's presence?

GABRIEL: It's something I am privileged to do daily.

ZACHARIAH: You are not supposed to be in here.

GABRIEL: You don't need to be afraid, Zacharias. Your prayer has been heard, and your wife Elizabeth will bear you a son.

Pause.

Zachariah no longer shows fear. He starts to laugh. The angel looks away.

GABRIEL: Why do you ask for something, if you don't believe you will receive it?

ZACHARIAH: I asked because I made a promise to my wife.

GABRIEL: Is there anything too hard for God?

ZACHARIAH: I am a High Priest according to the order of Melchizedek. I am not allowed to doubt what the God of our ancestors can do.

GABRIEL: Do you believe that God can give you a son in your old age?

ZACHARIAH: Me, without a doubt. I am a man. But my wife is way past the age of producing eggs for childbearing.

Pause.

GABRIEL: God will give you and your wife Elizabeth a son. You will call his name John, and you will have joy and gladness, and many will rejoice at his birth. For he will be great in the sight of the Lord, and shall drink neither wine nor strong drink. He will also be filled with the Holy Spirit, even from his mother's womb. And he will turn many of the children of Israel to the Lord their God. He will also go before Him in the spirit and power of Elijah, 'to turn the hearts of the fathers to the children,' and the disobedient to the wisdom of the just, to make ready a people prepared for the Lord.

ZACHARIAH: Why have you come to punish us with false hope? How will I know that what you have said is true?

GABRIEL: I am Gabriel, who stands in the presence of God and was sent to speak to you and bring you this good news. Because of your doubt, you will be unable to speak until these things come to past.

Gabriel turns to leave. Zachariah opens his mouth to respond, but there are no words, no sound. He only watches in silence as Gabriel exit.

Zachariah exits the temple. He meets the other two priests outside.

PRIEST 1: We were getting a little concerned you were in there too long.

Zachariah again tries to speak, but there are no words.

PRIEST 2: What happened to you in there?

Again Zachariah opens his mouth but nothing.

PRIEST 1: Did you see a vision?

Zachariah waves them off and exits. Both priest look at each other.

LIGHTS FADE

The Chosen Virgin

SCENE 5

LIGHTS UP

Mary and her mother Anna are gathering sticks to build a fire.

ANNA: Joseph seems to be a good man.

MARY: Seems to be!?

ANNA: Are you concerned?

MARY: That somewhere beneath the sweetness lies a little devil. Shouldn't I be?

ANNA: I think Joseph is a good choice for you, and you shouldn't allow yourself to be so concerned.

MARY: I am still young, mother. I have a lot to learn, like what it means exactly to be betrothed to a man.

Anna laughs.

ANNA: It is threefold. The engagement, which is the formal agreement made by the fathers; the betrothal is that ceremony you had where mutual promises are made and then marriage which takes place one year later when the bridegroom comes at an unexpected time for his bride.

MARY: Does that mean I am not allowed to see anyone else?

ANNA: Yes. You are under an obligation of faithfulness that can only be broken through divorce.

MARY: I thought divorce was only for the married.

ANNA: Betrothal is a binding agreement.

MARY: That's comforting.

ANNA: Have you seen Joseph lately?

MARY: I'm supposed to meet him by the brook this evening. Just before the sun sets.

ANNA: Sounds romantic.

MARY: Uhm!

ANNA: I'm gonna go start dinner.

MARY: I will join you shortly. I need some time to think.

Anna takes the sticks from Mary.

ANNA: Take all the time you need.

Anna exits.

Gabriel appears behind Mary.

GABRIEL: Rejoice, highly favored one, the Lord is with you; blessed are you among women!

Mary turns to see Gabriel. She falls to the ground afraid.

MARY: Who are you?

GABRIEL: Do not be afraid, Mary. For you have found favor with God.

MARY: I am troubled by your words.

GABRIEL: Behold, you will conceive in your womb and bring forth a Son, and shall call His name Jesus. He will be great, and will be called the Son of the Highest; and the Lord God will give Him the throne of His father David. And He will reign over the house of Jacob forever, and of His kingdom there will be no end.

MARY: How will this happen, since I don't know a man?

GABRIEL: Do you believe that all things are possible with God?

MARY: Yes, I do believe.

GABRIEL: The Holy Spirit will come upon you, and the power of the Highest will overshadow you; therefore, also, that Holy One who is to be born will be called the Son of God.

MARY: Please give me some confirmation that this will happen.

GABRIEL: Elizabeth your relative has also conceived a son in her old age; and this is now the sixth month for her who was called to be barren. For with God, nothing will be impossible.

MARY: Behold the maidservant of the Lord! Let it be to me according to your word.

Gabriel exits with a smile.

Anna enters and looks around.

ANNA: Mary, who are you talking to?

Pause.

ANNA: Mary, are you all right?

MARY: I need to go see my cousin Elizabeth.

ANNA: Do you know how to find her?

MARY: I think I remember the way.

ANNA: Do what you think you must, child, but please have some dinner first. It's a long journey.

They both exit.

LIGHTS OUT

The Confirmation

SCENE 6

LIGHTS UP

Elizabeth is quilting a baby shirt. Zachariah sits close by with a notepad and pen in his hand.

Elizabeth stops quilting and tries to speak to Zachariah with sign language.

Zachariah is obviously annoyed. He writes something, tears the page out and hands it to his wife.

ELIZABETH: *(reads)* I can hear. *(pause)* Sorry, Zachariah. It takes a little getting used to.

Pause.

ELIZABETH: It must really annoy you that everyone signs to you, not realizing that you are dumb but not deaf?

Zachariah shakes his head.

Elizabeth signs again, but this time teasingly.

Zachariah gives her a stern look.

Mary enters.

MARY: Cousin.

Elizabeth looks past Zachariah to see Mary coming in and instantly the quilt falls from her hands as she feels a sudden leap in her stomach.

Zachariah runs to her, unsure of what is happening.

ELIZABETH: It's okay. I'm fine. The baby isn't due for another two months.

Zachariah is beckoning at her to see what just happened. Elizabeth points past him at Mary.

Zachariah waves Mary closer.

ELIZABETH: Please give us a minute, Zachariah.

Zachariah nods.

MARY: Hi, cousin.

Zachariah can only wave as he leaves.

MARY: That's a bit strange. Usually Zachariah has much to say.

ELIZABETH: Yes, usually.

A beat.

Mary looks at Elizabeth's protruding stomach.

Elizabeth takes her hand and lays it on her stomach.

MARY: It is true.

ELIZABETH: The Lord has dealt kindly with us. He has taken away my reproach among the people. It was so overwhelming, I spent the first five months with the Lord just seeking Him for direction and the destiny of this child.

MARY: I am so happy for you, Elizabeth.

ELIZABETH: If God can do this for me, imagine what He will do for you.

MARY: That's why I am here.

ELIZABETH: I know. Blessed are you among women, Mary, and blessed is the fruit of your womb. But why is this granted to me, that the mother of my Lord should come to me?

MARY: I had to see it for myself.

ELIZABETH: As soon as the voice of your greeting sounded in my ears, the babe leaped in my womb for joy. Mary, all you have to do is believe, and you will see the fulfillment of everything the Lord has said.

MARY: I have spent my life studying God's word. I would not dream that I would be chosen for its fulfillment. It still feels like a dream.

ELIZABETH: I have been there, but if God brings you to it, He will surely bring you through it.

Pause.

MARY: My soul magnifies the Lord
And my spirit has rejoiced in God my savior.
For He has regarded the lowly state of His maidservant;
For behold, henceforth all generations will call me blessed.

For He who is mighty has done great things for me,
and holy *is* His name.
And His mercy *is* on those who fear Him from generation to generation.
He has shown strength with His arm;
He has scattered *the* proud in the imagination of their hearts.

He has put down the mighty from *their* thrones,
and exalted *the* lowly.
He has filled *the* hungry with good things,
and *the* rich He has sent away empty.
He has helped His servant Israel,
in remembrance of *His* mercy,
as He spoke to our fathers,
to Abraham and to his seed forever.

ELIZABETH: You were always a woman of Scripture. How long will you be staying?

MARY: I would love to be here to see the fulfillment of your promise.

ELIZABETH: My doors are never closed for you, Mary. You know that.

They fall into an embrace.

LIGHTS FADE

Birth of John

SCENE 7

Sound of a baby crying.

LIGHTS UP

Elizabeth is holding her baby in her arms. Zachariah proudly sits close to them.

Mary brings Elizabeth a glass of water.

MARY: The whole neighborhood is outside waiting to see the child, your child.

ELIZABETH: He will be circumcised today.

MARY: And also named. God has shown you great mercy, my cousin. You should name him after his father Zachariah.

ELIZABETH: No. He will be called John.

MARY: But there is no one among our relatives who is called by that name. I'm sure Zachariah would not mind naming him Zachariah.

Mary signs to Zachariah, who rolls his eyes.

ELIZABETH: Remember, he is just unable to speak. He hears perfectly well.

MARY: Oh, I keep forgetting. What name would you like to give your son?

Zachariah scribbles something and hands it to Mary.

MARY: *(reads)* His name is John.

Pause.

MARY: I guess you have both talked about this already.

ELIZABETH: Just the same as the angel told you the name you should give to your Son, he also told us the name we should give to ours.

MARY: That is super cool.

Elizabeth holds John out, and Zachariah takes him. He looks at his child and smiles.

ZACHARIAH: My child. *(Shocked that the words came out)*

Mary and Elizabeth are astonished.

ELIZABETH: Now I know that this child is destined to be great.

ZACHARIAH: Blessed *is* the Lord God of Israel, for He has visited and redeemed His people,
and has raised up a horn of salvation for us in the house of His servant David,
as He spoke by the mouth of His holy prophets,
who *have been* since the world began,
that we should be saved from our enemies and from the hand of all who hate us,
to perform the mercy *promised* to our fathers and to remember His holy covenant,
the oath which He swore to our father Abraham:

To grant us that we, being delivered from the hand of our enemies, might serve Him without fear,
in holiness and righteousness before Him all the days of our life.
And you, child, will be called the prophet of the Highest;
for you will go before the face of the Lord to prepare His ways,
to give knowledge of salvation to His people by the remission of their sins,
through the tender mercy of our God,
with which the Dayspring from on high has visited us;
to give light to those who sit in darkness and the shadow of death,
to guide our feet into the way of peace.

ELIZABETH: The voice of Prophecy has been silent for 400 years.

MARY: Until now!

ELIZABETH: Mary, be cautious and trust the God of our ancestors. The road which lies before you will not be an easy one.

MARY: The thought have robbed me of much sleep, but I must face my destiny.

ELIZABETH: My prayers are with you.

MARY: Thank you, Elizabeth. I'm going to need it.

    LIGHTS OUT

Act II

The Chosen Father

SCENE 1

LIGHTS UP

Joseph sits on a stone waiting.

Mary enters, strolling across the stage not realizing Joseph is sitting close by. He sees her before she sees him and quickly goes to meet her.

Joseph is overjoyed to see her, but there is a mixed expression on her face.

JOSEPH: I have been coming to this spot six days a week for two months waiting for your return, and you seem very disappointed to see me.

MARY: I'm glad to see you, Joseph, .it's just that I have some news you might not take very well.

JOSEPH: Should I sit down?

MARY: No. I saw people leaving the city in droves. What's going on?

JOSEPH: You haven't heard?

MARY: Heard what?

JOSEPH: Caesar Augustus has issued a decree that the whole world should be registered. Everyone in their own country.

MARY: So, you will be leaving for Bethlehem?

JOSEPH: We will be leaving for Bethlehem. Me and my betrothed wife.

MARY: It's amazing how one man speaks, and the world responds.

JOSEPH: We both know what Caesar did to be on that throne. He is a powerful man.

MARY: Yet, he can't save the people from themselves.

JOSEPH: Let's be careful how we talk about those in authority.

Pause.

JOSEPH: How long do you want me to pretend that I don't know something is terribly wrong?

MARY: I have been chosen, Joseph, for something quite unnatural. There is no way I could explain it for a human mind to understand. It takes faith in God only to be able to accept what I am about to tell you.

JOSEPH: And I do have faith. You already know this.

MARY: I was visited by an angel who told me I would bear God's son in my own womb.

Pause.

JOSEPH: Well, I guess as soon as we are officially married we can start working on that.

MARY: I am pregnant now!

Pause. Longer pause.

JOSEPH: It sounds like you just said, I am pregnant now.

MARY: I did.

Pause.

JOSEPH: Is that why you were gone for two months?

MARY: I was with my cousin. She now has a son.

JOSEPH: Which cousin?

MARY: Elizabeth.

JOSEPH: Elizabeth is an old woman. Are you on drugs?

MARY: Do you believe that God can do the impossible?

33

JOSEPH: Yes, but surely not the ridiculous. How can you be pregnant, Mary, without knowing a man? And how can you know a man, when you are betroth to me. It's a binding contract. How could you do this?

MARY: I am still a virgin, Joseph.

JOSEPH: A pregnant virgin? You want me to believe that you are a pregnant virgin?

MARY: There is no other way for me to say it.

JOSEPH: Do you see the word DUMB written across my forehead?

MARY: Joseph, please.

JOSEPH: You have put us in quite a predicament, Mary.

MARY: We are witnesses to a miraculous conception by the Holy Spirit, Joseph.

JOSEPH: Be careful. Blaspheming against the Holy Ghost is an unforgivable sin.

MARY: I am telling you the truth.

JOSEPH: Even if I accepted that as truth, what will people say? What will they think? Our families will be dishonoured. Especially in light of the fact that people have been spreading rumors that you are sleeping with a Roman soldier.

MARY: But you know that is not true.

JOSEPH: Does it matter what I know? Does it even matter now what I think?

MARY: It matters to me. If I never needed you before, Joseph, I need you now.

Pause.

JOSEPH: I can't. This is too much. But I love you enough not to make a public example of you, Mary, so we will do away with this contract quietly.

MARY: What are you saying?

JOSEPH: I thought that was obvious. The wedding is off.

MARY: I really thought that if anyone else believed me, it would have been you.

Pause.

JOSEPH: Why don't you just come straight with me? I think I deserve that much. Just tell me the truth.

MARY: I did.

Mary steps past him and exits.

JOSEPH: This woman thinks I'm a fool. Sensitive perhaps, but not a fool.

He sits on the stone.

JOSEPH: What do I do now? If I divorce her quietly, then I leave her to bear the shame alone. She would doubt my love for her. My God, I don't know what to do. I can't go through with a marriage to someone who has been unfaithful and yet, why does a quiet divorce feel like the wrong choice.

He pulls his knees up to his chest and folds his hands around them, resting his head on his knee.

Gabriel enters and stands a little way off.

GABRIEL: Joseph!

Joseph looks over at him.

JOSEPH: Do I know you?

GABRIEL: Son of David. Why are you sad?

JOSEPH: My heart is troubled.

GABRIEL: You have no reason to be afraid to take to you Mary as your wife. What she told you is true. That which is conceived in her is of the Holy Spirit. She will bring forth a Son, and you shall call His name JESUS, for He will save His people from their sins.

JOSEPH: Who are you?

GABRIEL: I am just a messenger.

Pause.

JOSEPH: A son?

GABRIEL: He will save the world from the penalty, the power and the presence of sin.

JOSEPH: The Messiah?

GABRIEL: Mary needs you, Joseph. Until this point, you were an ordinary man who would have been forgotten after you die. Now your name will be remembered through all generations as the man who fathered God's Son.

JOSEPH: This is a dream.

GABRIEL: The Lord spoke through the Prophets many years ago about this day. Joseph, you have been chosen. It's time to face your destiny.

Gabriel exits. Joseph gets to his feet.

JOSEPH: Mary was speaking the truth.

He quickly exits in the same direction Mary went.

LIGHTS OUT

The In Keeper

SCENE 2

LIGHTS UP

Mary, in an advanced stage of pregnancy, sits waiting.

Joseph enters.

JOSEPH: I'm sorry to keep you waiting so long, dear, but the line was really long. I did tell you to remain in Nazareth.

MARY: And be the subject of gossip? I don't think so.

JOSEPH: I am glad for the company, but now I feel insensitive to have agreed for you to come.

MARY: Did you get it done?

JOSEPH: Yes, I just registered us both.

MARY: That's good, because I have some really bad news.

Joseph goes to her side. She is rubbing her stomach.

MARY: I can't make it back.

JOSEPH: What do you mean?

MARY: I can't make the journey back, Joseph. This baby is coming today.

JOSEPH: Can't you hold him like you hold everything else?

MARY: I don't think it works like that. We need somewhere to stay.

JOSEPH: Everybody who comes from the house and lineage of David is here today, and will be here for a few days. There is no way we're going to find an available room to rent.

MARY: Well, then, you should start praying, because I need a room. I'm not breaking water in the streets. There's an inn over there *(points Stage Right)* and one over there *(points Stage Left)*. Get us a room now Joseph. Please!

Joseph paces back and forth a bit. He decides to approach far Stage Left. He knocks on a door.

A short Plump Man eventually answers.

MAN: Greetings. What can I do for you?

JOSEPH: My wife is having a baby, and we need a room.

MAN: I am filled to capacity.

JOSEPH: Can you at least check to see if you have a room available?

MAN: Are you implying that I don't know my own Inn?

JOSEPH: No, sir. I'm just desperate and think it would do no harm to double check.

MAN: I love money. Turning people away gives me no pleasure whatsoever, especially considering how slow this year has been. God bless Caesar, if I had room to hold more, I would gladly take you and your wife, but as I said before, we are filled to capacity.

JOSEPH: What do I do?

MAN: Well now, that would be your problem. Not mine!

The Plump Man closes the door in Joseph's face.

Mary grabs her stomach, her face twisted in pain.

Joseph runs to her side.

JOSEPH: Whatever you do, Mary, do not push.

MARY: Get me off this street, Joseph. Please.

JOSEPH: God, I know this is something great, but I don't really understand it, and it makes me nervous. Please help us.

Joseph goes far Stage Right and knocks on another door.

MAURINE answers.

MAURINE: Yes.

JOSEPH: We need a room. Please.

MAURINE: We have no more available room.

JOSEPH: Please help us. Please. My wife is about to give birth. Is there anything you can do for us?

Maurine looks past Joseph at Mary twisted and yelping in pain.

MAURINE: Let me talk to my husband.

Maurine closes the door for a beat.

Joseph goes for his wife. Maurine comes back out and closes the door behind her.

MAURINE: Follow me.

Maurine leads them offstage. A beat.

The door opens, and the INNKEEPER steps out. He looks around, walks further Stage Left still looking.

Maurine speedily returns and heads for the door.

INNKEEPER: Hold up there, missy. What are you doing?

MAURINE: They need some stuff; blankets, alcohol, sterilizers ---

INNKEEPER: Where did you put them? I told you there was no room.

MAURINE: They are in the manger.

INNKEEPER: Whose manger? My manger?

MAURINE: Would you had rather I left them on the streets?

39

INNKEEPER: When will you stop trying to save the world, woman?

MAURINE: Would you want your son to be born on the streets?

Pause.

MAURINE: I thought so. Either you help me or keep out of my way.

Maurine disappears through the door.

INNKEEPER: *(shakes his head)* Women! They got our ribs, but they don't got our heart.

Innkeeper exits behind his wife.

LIGHTS FADE

The Shepherds

SCENE 3

LIGHTS UP

Three Shepherds stand at Center Stage looking out over the audience.

MARK: I still can't believe it, of all the shepherds in this country, I was chosen.

PAUL: Eventually, you will get used to it.

MARK: Get used to being counted among the few who watch over the sheep that are sacrificed in the temple! Are you kidding?

RAYMOND: You are new, Mark. After you have done it for a while, it just starts to feel natural.

MARK: Whatever it is I am feeling now, I really don't want to lose it. I see how you guys just go through the motions of each day, but I don't want that to happen to me.

PAUL: It happens to the best of us.

MARK: It's the reasons why so many marriages fail.

RAYMOND: Do you really want to go there, son?

Pause.

MARK: I'm just saying, being few chosen from many should never feel 'normal' or 'natural.'

Gabriel enters.

The Shepherds see him and raise their staffs in defense, shaking at the site of this strange person.

PAUL: I-I-Identify yourself.

GABRIEL: Why are you afraid?

RAYMOND: You are unlike any ordinary man that we have ever seen.

GABRIEL: You do not need to be afraid. I bring you some good news that will be to all people. For there is born to you this day in the city of David, a Saviour, who is Christ the Lord.

RAYMOND: Can this really be true?

GABRIEL: Look for this sign: you will find a Babe wrapped in swaddling clothes and lying in a manger.

Other Angels appear all over the stage.

GABRIEL: Glory to God in the highest, and on earth, peace, goodwill toward all men.

They sing the 'Hallelujah Chorus'

The Shepherds fall to their faces.

The Angels leave at the end of the song.

MARK: We have seen God. We are going to die.

PAUL: You talked earlier about being privileged, my young friend. But if you knew Scripture, none of this would seem strange to you.

MARK: What are you talking about?

RAYMOND: The words of the Prophet **ISAIAH**: "For unto us a child is born, unto us a son is given: and the government shall be upon his shoulder: and his name shall be called Wonderful, Counsellor, The mighty God, The everlasting Father, The Prince of Peace."

PAUL: The emperor, as great as he is, can only give peace from war on land and on sea.

RAYMOND: But the Messiah will give peace from passion, grief, and envy.

MARK: Who is this Messiah?

PAUL: The one who was promised to our ancestors by God the Father. He will come to undo what Adam, the first father, did.

RAYMOND: We are not just privileged to watch over the sacrificial sheep, we have just received the announcement of the coming into this world of the Shepherd.

Pause.

MARK: Then we should go to Bethlehem. See this thing that has come to pass, which the Lord has made known to us.

PAUL: We will need gifts.

They exit as

LIGHTS FADE

King Herod & The Wise Men

SCENE 4

LIGHTS UP

King Herod is seated on his throne feeding on grapes from a nearby tray.

A hired servant attends to his feet.

One of his Advisers enters and bows.

ADVISER: My king.

KING HEROD: What is it?

ADVISER: There are Wise Men standing in the foyer. They say they have been traveling from the east in search of a king.

KING HEROD: Why are they searching for me? Everyone knows where to find me.

ADVISER: You are not the king they seek, sir.

Pause. King Herod stops eating. He waves off his servant who quickly leaves.

KING HEROD: Is there another king besides me?

ADVISER: I think it's best if you spoke with them personally.

KING HEROD: So bring them in!

ADVISER: There is a great company of them my Lord.

KING HEROD: Then bid the two more knowledgeable and capable ones to come.

The Adviser nods and exits.

A beat.

Two Wise men enter. Their names are Balthasar and Caspar.

BALTHASAR: Mighty King Herod. My name is Balthasar, and this is my companion Caspar.

CASPAR: Your fame has stretched far and wide, and we bring you greetings from the east.

KING HEROD: And what would star gazers want in this part of the world?

BALTHASAR: We seek the one who has been born King of the Jews. We have seen His star in the East, and have come to worship Him.

KING HEROD: Tell me more about this king.

CASPAR: Careful study of Daniel and the ancient prophets tells of a coming Messiah. Daniel himself formed the order of the Magi and instructed our ancestors to watch for this Messiah.

KING HEROD: Is that what this is about? Ancient writings of prophetic significance?

BALTHASAR: We have dedicated our lives to the study of prophecies. For centuries, the world has been looking for a Messiah; the one promised to us by God the Father.

KING HEROD: And you think the Messiah has come, now, in our time?

CASPAR: Not just in our time, but here in Jerusalem; the center of the earth.

Pause.

KING HEROD: It seems I am ignorant to all this and must consult with my advisers to see how best we can assist you in finding what you are looking for. Can you wait just a little while with your other companions?

BALTHASAR: We will wait.

The Wise Men exit.

The Adviser returns.

KING HEROD: Do you know of this King that the magi speak about?

ADVISER: It's a legend spoken of by people of old.

KING HEROD: A legend? You think these men of Persia would travel halfway across the world for a legend?

ADVISER: Not everyone believes what is written in the ancient scrolls.

KING HEROD: Does that make it any less valid?

ADVISER: No, my king.

KING HEROD: Tell me about this King and choose your words carefully, Adviser.

ADVISER: I think the Priest and Scribes can relay more accurate information.

KING HEROD: Bring me a representative of both.

ADVISER: I already did. I will send them in.

The Adviser leaves and a PRIEST & SCRIBE enters, they bow.

KING HEROD: There are wise men standing in my foyer inquiring about a King to be born king of the Jews. What do you know about this?

SCRIBE: Scriptures tell of a Child born to a virgin who would save the people from their sin; the Christ-child, as some have interpreted it to mean.

KING HEROD: Where is this Christ supposed to be born?

SCRIBE: In Bethlehem of Judea.

PRIEST: It is written: "But you, Bethlehem, in the land of Judea, are not the least among the rulers of Judah; for out of you shall come a Ruler who will shepherd My people Israel."

KING HEROD: I am Israel's shepherd.

SCRIBE: We know that, my king, but unfortunately not everyone believes that.

KING HEROD: How then do I make everyone believe?

Pause.

PRIEST: If there is found to be a Christ-child, then the order of things as we know it will be permanently disrupted.

KING HEROD: You don't believe in the Prophecies?

PRIEST: We are priests in Gods house. Of course we do, but we also believe we are far from seeing its fulfillment. Many have come claiming to be, but was not. This time will be no different.

SCRIBE: If the Messiah was here, then I think as Priest and Scribes we would have received some confirmation in our spirits. What you face today, my king, is an outright threat to your throne?

KING HEROD: And what should a king do about such a threat?

PRIEST: That is the question that you must answer, my king.

Pause.

KING HEROD: Send the wise men in on your way out.

They bow and exit.

Balthasar and Caspar return.

KING HEROD: At what time did this star first appear?

BALTHASAR: It's hard to tell.

KING HEROD: You will find the Child you seek in Bethlehem. Search carefully, and when you have found Him, I charge you to bring back word to me that I may come and worship Him also.

CASPAR: We will stop by on our way back. Thank you.

They bow and exit.

King Herod remains on his throne deep in thought.

LIGHTS FADE

The Manger

SCENE 5

LIGHTS UP

***SONG:** Mary Did You Know*

Mary sits behind a feeding trough where baby Jesus is lying.

Joseph kneels by her sid,e and they are both looking at the baby and smiling.

Maurine leads three Shepherds in. It is a moment of awe, unbelief, and worship. They bow and offer gifts to Mary & Joseph, who places them around where Jesus is.

The Wise Men appear from another direction. They point towards the sky apparently at where the star has stopped moving, realizing it now rest over the very spot.

Mary is in tears to see the well-learned men approaching with gifts and bowing in worship to her Baby.

Gabriel and a host of angels appear.

The Wise Men offer their gifts one after the other.

The Innkeeper enters. He joins with his wife, astonished at the scene unfolding before him.

Mary takes Jesus, wrapped in swaddling clothes (loose clothes) and hold Him close to her bosom on the last line of the song (--- this sleeping child you're holding --- is the great I Am)

BALTHASAR: What is the name of the child?

MARY: His name is Jesus.

CASPAR: God with us!

Pause.

MARY: You have blessed us with three gifts that I believe are symbolic to the journey which lies before us. Gold to represent His Royalty, Frankincense His priesthood and Myrrh His death.

BALTHASAR: It is no secret to those who study Scriptures. Isaiah makes it too plain to even be repeated here and now. Today we celebrate the birth of our Messiah. No need to think about anything else at this point.

JOSEPH: Well said.

MARY: You traveled many months to get here?

CASPAR: And we have an even longer journey ahead of us. King Herod charged us to bring him back word when we found the Child, but God has shown us his true intentions. We take a different road home.

MARY: Thank you.

BALTHASAR: Be careful.

The Wise Men leaves.

MARK: We will speak about this day until the day we die, and our children and children's children will tell this story.

The Shepherds shake the hands of Mary and Joseph, then exits.

Maurine hugs Mary and Joseph.

MARY: Thank you.

MAURINE: Will you two be okay?

MARY: Yes.

JOSEPH: We must go now. We have a long journey ahead of us.

MAURINE: Take care of yourselves, and baby Jesus and please feel free to visit us again, whenever.

MARY: Okay.

Joseph shakes the Innkeepers hand as they exit.

The Innkeeper and Maurine watch them leave.

LIGHTS FADE

The Temple

SCENE 6

LIGHTS UP

Simeon enters and walks to the altar. He strikes a match and lights two candles.

Anna, an elderly widow, enters from an adjoining room.

ANNA: Simeon! I did not expect you until tomorrow.

SIMEON: I was led here by the Spirit.

ANNA: What reason would the Spirit have to bring you here at this hour?

SIMEON: We will find out soon enough, I guess.

Pause.

SIMEON: I have been meaning to talk to you, Anna. Don't you ever consider going home?

ANNA: This is my home.

SIMEON: This is a temple. Home is where your family is.

ANNA: My husband was my only family. Since he died, the only family I have known is here.

SIMEON: Your husband died when you were 25. You have spent almost a lifetime here just fasting and praying.

ANNA: And I have never once complained, Simeon. We all have a calling and a purpose. Mine is to be here.

SIMEON: I just need to know that you are content with this lifestyle.

ANNA: I am.

SIMEON: Good. I need some water to wash the altar and prepare it for a sacrifice. I will also need the circumcision bowl and utensils.

ANNA: On it.

Anna exits.

SIMEON: Loyalty, without question. Such a rare trait these days.

Joseph and Mary enter.

Simeon's back is turned to them, but somehow he senses their presence. He turns to face them.

SIMEON: Lord God Almighty.

JOSEPH: Our Son is of the age to be circumcised.

SIMEON: What is the name of this Child?

JOSEPH: His name is Jesus.

SIMEON: A name given by angels. Every male who opens the womb shall be called holy to the Lord. A pair of turtledoves or two young pigeons. Have you brought these?

JOSEPH: Yes.

SIMEON: But I must ask, why would the One who has come to fulfill the law be subjected to it?

JOSEPH: In being obedient to the law, every aspect of it will be fulfilled. Jesus was not born in sin, but He will identify Himself with sinners to save all sinners.

SIMEON: I was promised by the Holy Spirit that I would not see death before I have seen the Lord.

Simeon takes the Child and raises Him to Heaven.

SIMEON: Lord, now you will let Your servant depart in peace, according to Your word; for my eyes have seen Your salvation, which You have prepared before the face of all peoples, a light to bring revelation to the Gentiles and the glory of Your people Israel.

Simeon hands the baby to Mary.

SIMEON: Behold, this Child is destined for the fall and rising of many in Israel, and for a sign which will be spoken against. A sword will pierce through your own soul also, that the thoughts of many hearts may be revealed.

MARY: What do you mean?

SIMEON: Mothering the Messiah will both be a great privilege and a great burden.

Anna enters with the circumcision instruments and a bowl of water, but as soon as she enters the room, something falls from her hands.

ANNA: I feel the presence of my God in this place. Who am I that I should be a witness to this marvelous thing?

A beat.

ANNA: Praise be to God, now I know, now I know that my Redeemer lives. For I have seen Him with my own eyes.

Pause.

Made in the USA
Las Vegas, NV
09 November 2023